AF746499

Name

Teacher

School

Are you ready to write?

Posture

Ensure your feet are flat on the floor and you are sitting well back in the chair.

Paper position

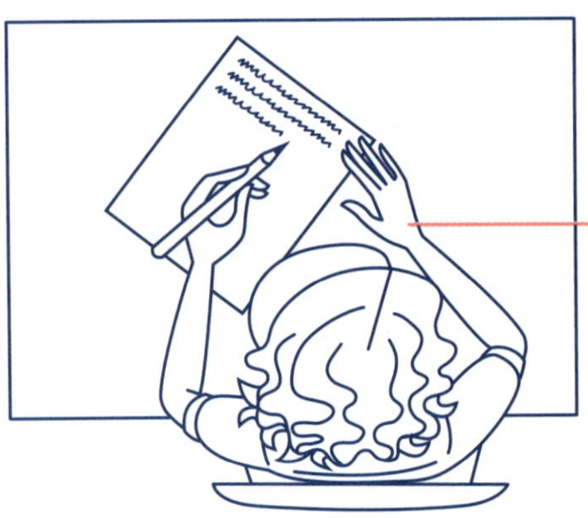

left-handed

Hold the paper with your non-writing hand.

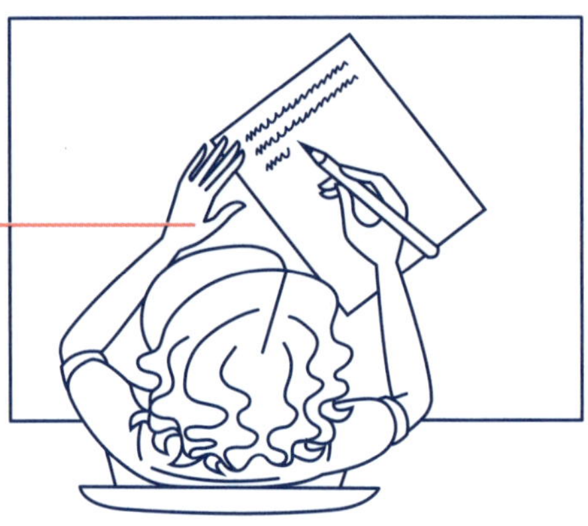

right-handed

Pencil grip

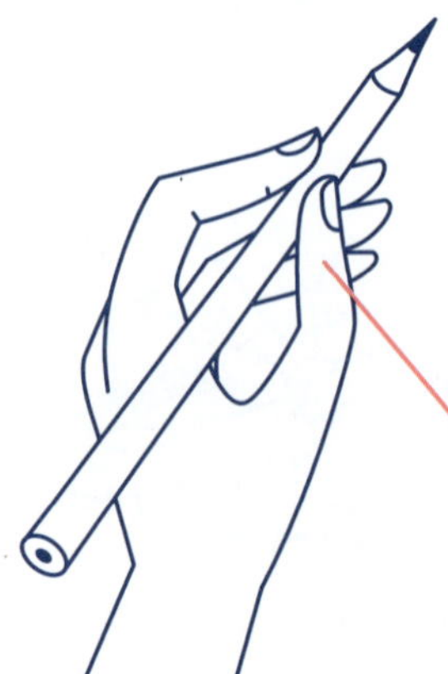

left-handed

Hold your pencil with one finger on top of the barrel.

Support the barrel with your thumb.

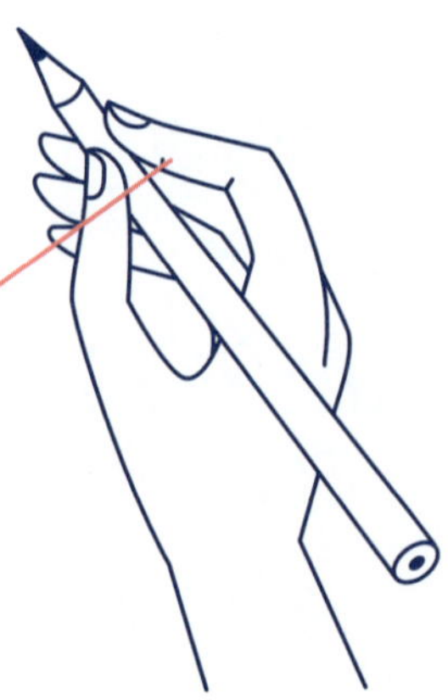

right-handed

Print script

Module 1: Space mysteries

Revise the print alphabet.

a b c d e f g h i j k l m n o p q r s t u v w x y z

Practise 'c' in the anti-clockwise pattern. Then copy the words.

crop circles geometric cereologist caused

acknowledge crops created cereal

Copy the text.

Crop circles are geometric patterns that mysteriously appear in crop fields. They are caused when areas of cereal crops are flattened. A cereologist is someone who studies crop circles. Though cereologists acknowledge that some crop circles are human-made, most believe that many of the patterns are created by time travellers or aliens.

Patterning exercises

Trace and repeat these patterns. Complete the rows.

Mysterious crop circles

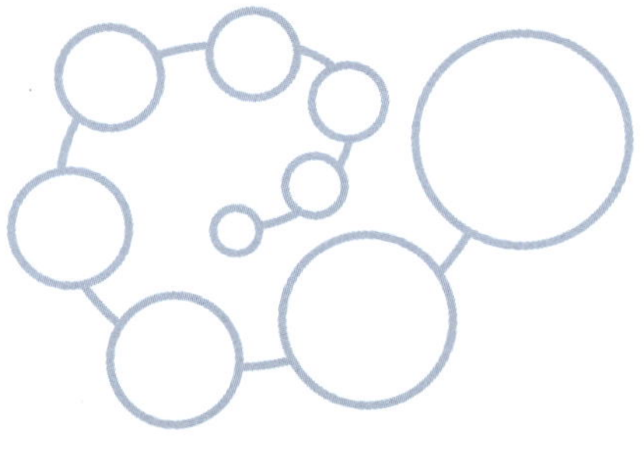

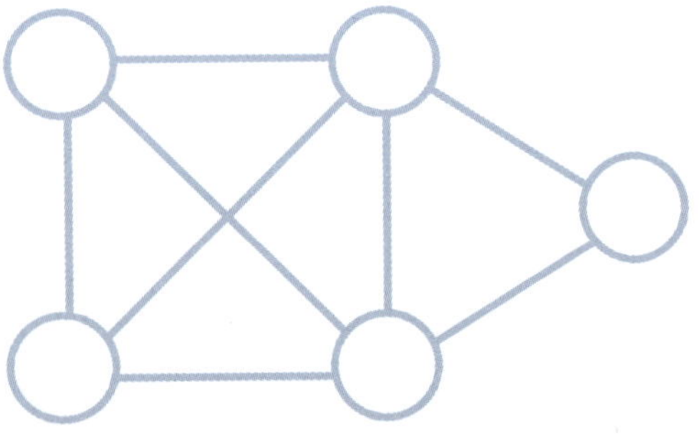

Capital letters

Revise the capital letters.

A B C D E F G H I J K L M N O P Q R S T U V W X Y Z

Rewrite each sentence in print, using capital letters in the correct places.

ufo is an abbreviation for 'unidentified flying object'.

many spectacular crop circles have appeared in wiltshire, in southern england.

dr horace drew is a well-known cereologist who believes crop circles are messages from aliens.

'the war of the worlds' is a famous science fiction novel by h. g. wells about a conflict between humankind and an extraterrestrial race.

my dad says, 'i'm a sceptic – i doubt that aliens exist'.

Labelling diagrams

Add events from the box to the timeline below, using print script.

1915 – A pilot fires on a UFO over London.

1947 – A UFO crashes in Roswell, New Mexico, in the USA.

1952 – Six discs circle above a town in Argentina.

1966 – A UFO hovers above Westall High School, Melbourne.

2006 – A saucer-shaped craft hovers above O'Hare Airport, USA.

Timeline of famous UFO sightings

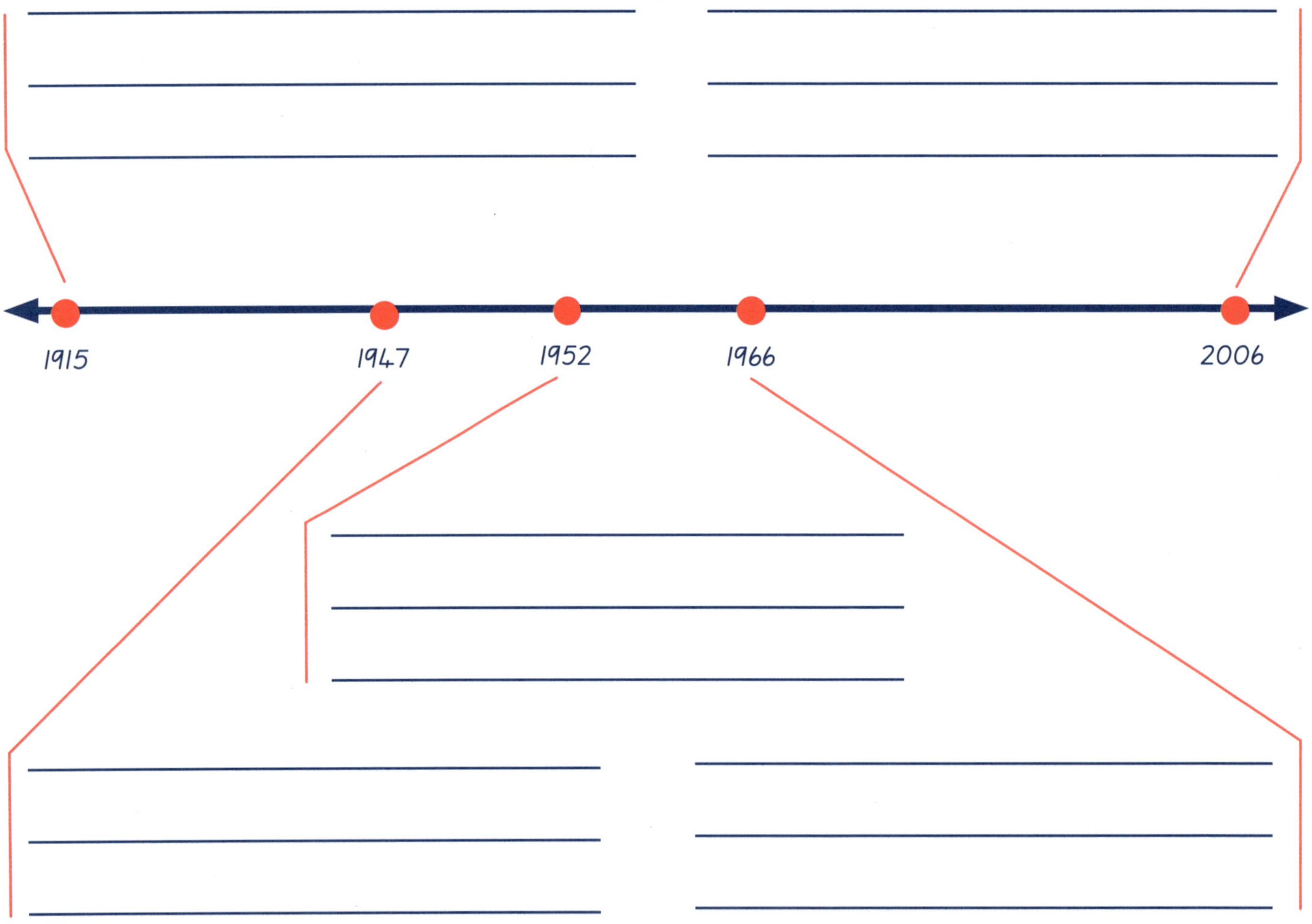

Numerals

Revise your numerals.

0 1 2 3 4 5 6 7 8 9 10 11 12 13 14 15 16 17 18 19 20

Copy these numerals and write the numeral names in cursive script.

5 five

50

500

50 000

500 000

5 000 000

Complete the table, using cursive script for numeral names.

500 050	
15 500	
	five thousand and fifteen
	five million, fifty thousand and five
50 050	
555	

Write the number from the table above that is more than six hundred thousand, in numerals and words.

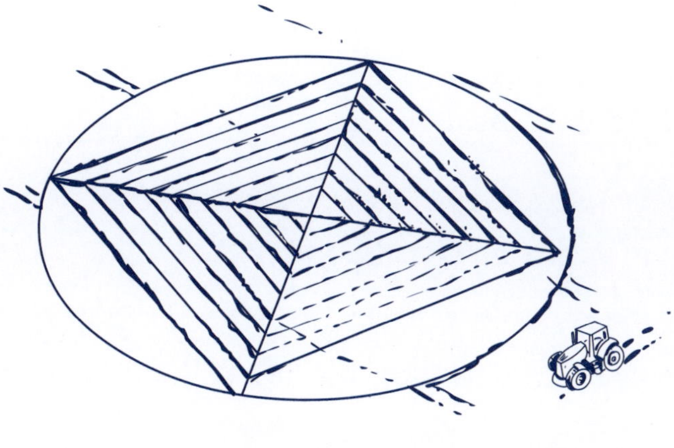

Revising drop-on joins

> *Drop-on joins are required when you join diagonally to shoulder letters.*

a c d g q

shoulder letters

Practise these letter pairs.

ea nc nd ig aq ia ec id ug iq ua ic ag

Copy these words. The dot reminds you when to use a drop-on join.

encounter flattened studying decoded equipment

saucer secrets landings binary advanced

messages ground images sending weather

Add a dot to indicate the drop-on joins in each word, then copy the words.

cause search planet explain claimed

increase feature sightings human images

liquid conspiracy geometric formation artistic

Self-assessment

Rate your use of drop-on joins.

☐ I have trouble remembering them.

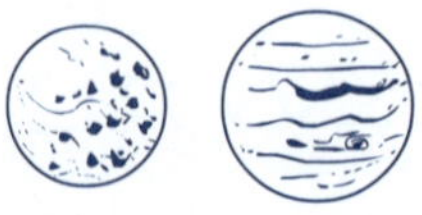

☐ I usually use them.

☐ I always use them.

Revising joins to ascenders

Remember which letters start with ascenders when you join from the previous letter.

b h k l t

letters with ascenders

Retrace one-third when joining diagonally to ascenders.

ub } $\frac{1}{3}$

Practise these letter pairs.

ib th ck ul et eb at cl ut ab tt it ct ub

Copy these words with joins to ascenders.

scientist circles alien contain Saturn planets

between travellers include countries clues

patterns elaborate usually researchers likely

sightings unidentified encounter believe

Convert the following words from print to cursive.

length subjects claimed world future general

belief false closing developed introduce bubbles

whales unknown nothing real scientific original

circular magnetic paranormal sceptical institute

get.ga/PMWA130

Revising joins to and from the letter 'f'

Remember: there are two forms of 'f' in cursive.

open 'f' modified 'f'

Pay attention to when open 'f' is used. Copy these words.

fascination flattened forward furniture future

fair flying field fear playful farmer formed

files former friendly full frequently helpful

Copy these words with modified 'f'.

unidentified defined handful peacefully definitely

afraid halfway scientific safely defences proof after

imperfections referred lifted powerful life information

Copy these words with double 'f'.

offers differentiating difference effect suffice

affect bluff chaff coffee effort unofficial

Slope

A consistent slope helps to keep your writing legible.

Copy the letters against the slope lines.

n p b d f g h i n q k l

Copy the letters, then draw in slope lines using a ruler.

q r a e h j l b d n m t l p

Copy the text, then check your slope. Use a ruler to draw in slope lines.

Crop circles are rarely found in Australia.

They are more likely to be found in the United Kingdom.

Self-assessment

How consistent is your slope?

☐ I need practice.

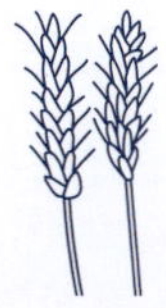

☐ I am usually consistent.

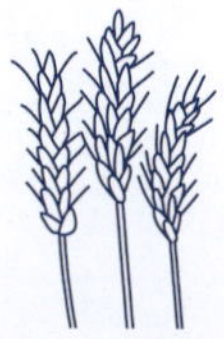

☐ I am very consistent!

Spacing

Write the text below using even spacing between letters and words.

An u nidentified fly ing ob ject, or UFO,

is a ny thing in the sk y that can not

be exp lained. In boo k s and movies, UFOs

often ap pear as saucer-shap ed craft.

Write the word 'circle' in cursive script to fill each word shape. Try to keep even spacing between letters.

Now write the word 'crop', copying the models. Circle the version of the word 'crop' you wrote with the most even spacing.

crop crop crop crop

Self-assessment

Rate your spacing.

☐ I need practice.

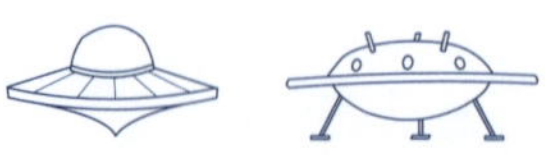

☐ It is usually appropriate.

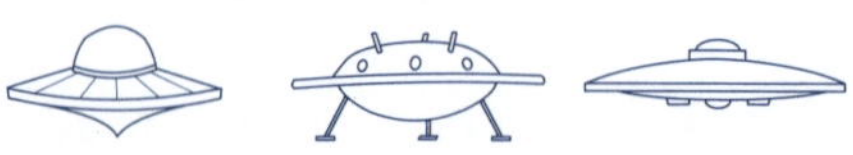

☐ It is always appropriate.

Size

Write the word 'craft' at different sizes. Try to maintain a consistent size and correct letter formation.

Trace.

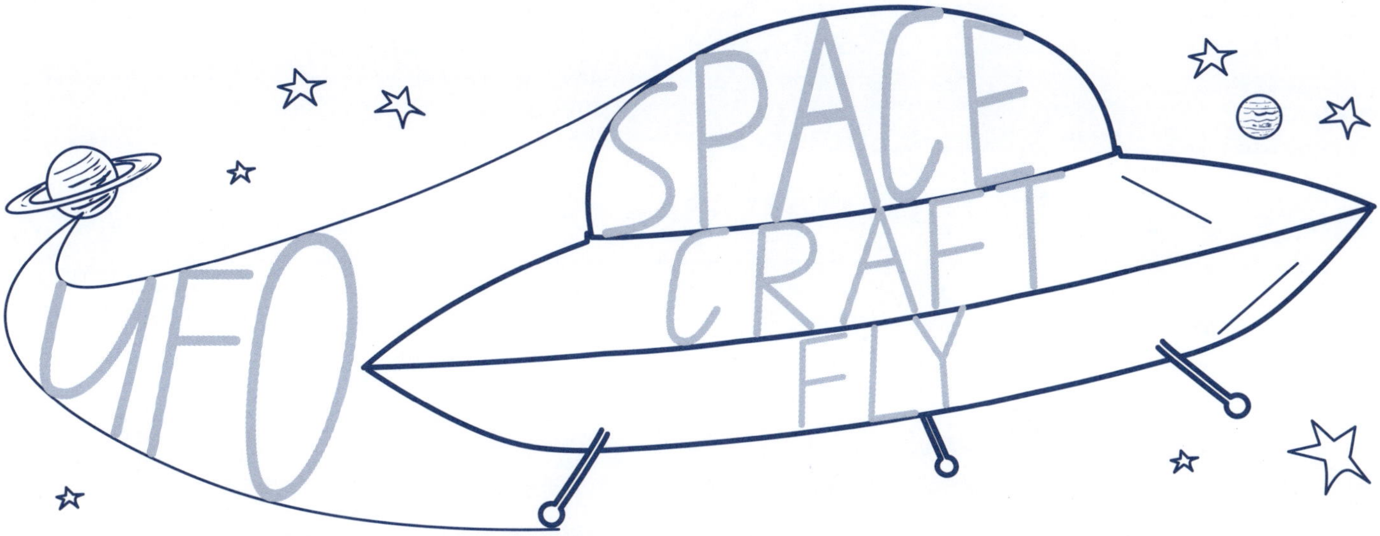

Fill the planets with the letters. Keep the size of your letters consistent within each planet.

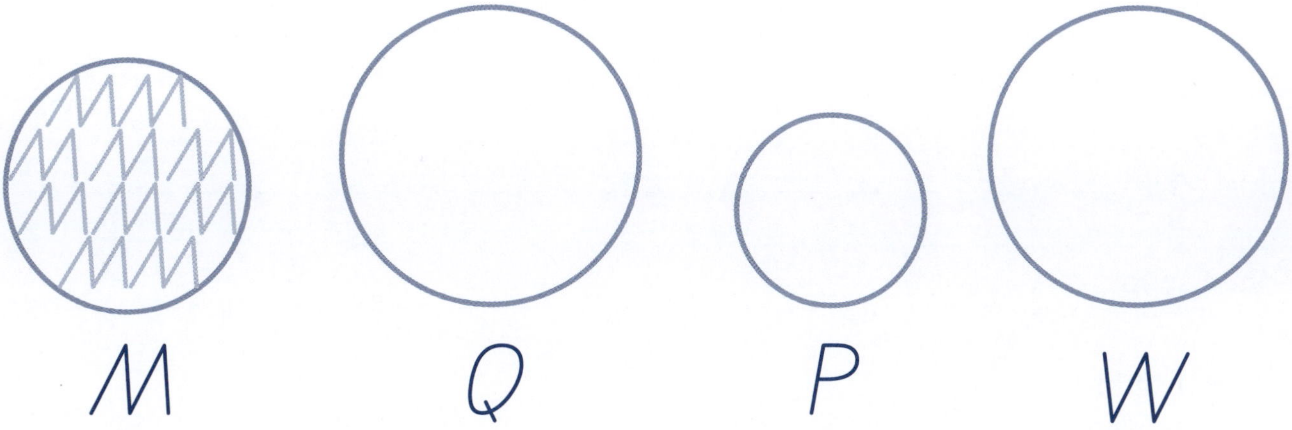

Speed and legibility

Can you write at speed but retain your legibility?

Work with a partner. How many times can you write the words 'flying saucer' in one minute?

get.ga/PMWA131

Print

flying saucer

_____ times

Cursive

flying saucer

_____ times

Capital letters

FLYING SAUCER

_____ times

My fastest script: ______________________

My neatest script: ______________________

My preferred script: ______________________

End-of-module evaluation: A UFO sighting

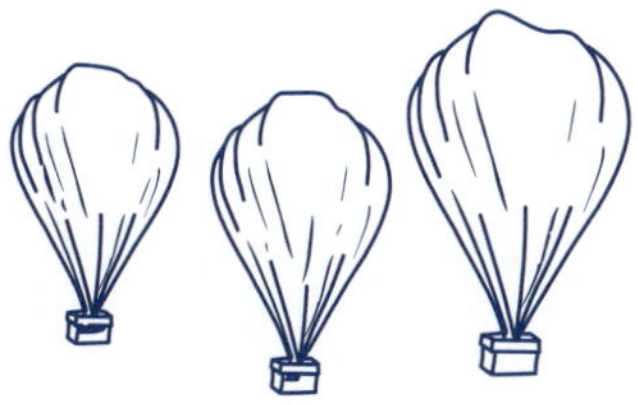

Copy the text, then evaluate your handwriting.

On that day in April, 1966, I remember being on the school oval with my friend, Annie. We were students of Westall High School, in the suburb of Clayton South, in Melbourne. Like many of our fellow students, we witnessed three balloon-like objects hovering above the ground. Afterwards, there was a circle of flattened grass left behind, about 5 metres in diameter. I believe the circle was burnt the next day by army officers. It was such a strange event, that I still remember it quite clearly today.

(Fictional recount based on real events)

Evaluation grid

	Student		Teacher	
Letters and words are a consistent size.	☐ Yes	☐ No	☐ Yes	☐ No
Letters and words are evenly spaced.	☐ Yes	☐ No	☐ Yes	☐ No
Slope is consistent.	☐ Yes	☐ No	☐ Yes	☐ No
All joins are accurate.	☐ Yes	☐ No	☐ Yes	☐ No
Handwriting is legible.	☐ Yes	☐ No	☐ Yes	☐ No

Print script

Revise the print alphabet.

a b c d e f g h i j k l m n o p q r s t u v w x y z

Find the letter 'm' in the clockwise pattern. Then copy the words.

m m m m

mysterious mythical monster may move

many some commonly more omen

Copy the text.

A cryptid is a mysterious, often mythical, creature, such as a beast or monster. It is not recognised by science and may or may not exist. Cryptids have been a source of speculation for many decades. The Loch Ness monster is one cryptid often written and spoken about. It has supposedly been sighted living in a lake in Scotland. While some are convinced of their existence, more commonly, cryptids are not believed to exist.

Patterning exercises

Trace the patterns and add some of your own.

The mythical Loch Ness monster

Capital letters

Revise the capital letters.

A B C D E F G H I J K L M N O P Q R S T U V

W X Y Z

Rewrite each sentence, using capital letters in the correct places.

Loch Ness, home to the mythical Loch Ness monster, is a large freshwater lake located in scotland. in 1934, British newspaper the daily mail published a now-famous photograph of what looked like the loch ness monster.

'Bigfoot' is a legendary ape-like beast rumoured to dwell in the forests of the Pacific Northwest in the USA. in october 1967, two men believed they discovered the footprints of Bigfoot in california, usa.

The Yeti is a mythical human-like creature thought to exist in the snowy Himalayan mountains, in the countries of tibet and nepal. A movie called 'the abominable snowman' is based on the legend of the yeti.

Labelling diagrams

Add labels to the diagram. Use print script.

The legendary Bigfoot

u

g

l

s

l

b

e

l

short neck   long arms   up to 2.75 metres tall   large eyes

gorilla-like head   bi-pedal (walks on two legs)

enormous feet   leaves giant footprints

Numerals

Revise your numerals.

10 20 30 40 50 60 70 80 90 100

Copy these numerals and write the numeral names in cursive script.

8 eight

18

88

808

8088

80 008

Write the missing numerals and numeral names.

800 080

18 800

eight thousand and eighteen

eight million, eighty thousand and eight

80 080

888

Copy these numbers and tricky numeral names.

40 forty 90 ninety 20 twenty 30 thirty

14 fourteen 50 fifty 12 twelve 100 one hundred

1 000 one thousand 1 000 000 one million

Write, in words, the number that is one less than one million.

Revising the letter 's'

A print 's' is used at the beginning of a word, and when there is no join to 's'.

Copy these words with a print 's'.

slope mystery straight sceptic story sightings

A print 's' is also used after a horizontal join.

Copy these words with horizontal joins to 's'.

closed first thirsty cost views pianos kilos claws

A modified 's' is used when there is a diagonal join to 's'.

Copy these words with a modified 's'.

case recognise visible existed mountainside

splashes ease snouts lakes monster

When writing double 's', make them look like twins.

get.ga/PMWA132

Copy these words with double 's'.

eeriness obsess grasses Loch Ness awareness classify

moss gloss floss across boss gross albatross

ISBN: 9780170403924

Revising double letters

Practise these double letter pairs.

bb cc dd ee ff gg kk ll mm nn

oo pp rr rr ss ss tt tt uu zz

ff Copy these words with modified double 'f'.

offside daffodil official stuffy suffer offer

rr rr Join double 'r' or leave them unjoined.

arrive arrive barrel barrel burrow burrow

ss Copy these words with horizontal joins to double 's'.

toss across crossing moss boss loss fossil

ss Copy these words with diagonal joins to double 's'.

miss dresses express dismiss glass guess

tt tt Cross double 't' with one stroke or two separate strokes.

butter butter bottle bottle kitten kitten

Revising horizontal joins

Horizontal joins are formed when joining from o, r, v or w. Remember not to dip too far.

or ✓ or ✗

Practise these letter pairs.

oi ra vi wa oy ry va wi og ru

Practise your horizontal joins. Copy these words.

mysterious Bigfoot known forests northwest

across throughout covered living bulldozer

report wooden however phenomenon scary

snowmen stories footprints turned monster

Underline the letter pairs in the words below that will have a horizontal join in cursive.
Prove your answers by writing the words in cursive.

ground brought tourist loch proof survived first

evidence encountered further European elongated royal

Slope

Practise maintaining a consistent slope. Trace and copy these slope patterns.

Copy the letters, then draw in slope lines.

b w y a e l h g j m p q d h

Copy the text, then check your slope. Use a ruler to draw in slope lines.

Bigfoot is also known as Sasquatch. Sasquatch means 'hairy giant' according to some indigenous North American legends. Many people claim to have seen the ape-like creature but no one has captured it or found its body. Bigfoot is described as being 2 to 2.75 metres tall with brown, black, red or white fur. Its large feet are said to be about 56 centimetres long.

Self-assessment

Rate the consistency of your slope.

☐ It is not consistent.

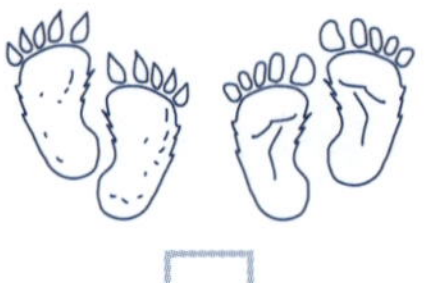

☐ It is mostly consistent.

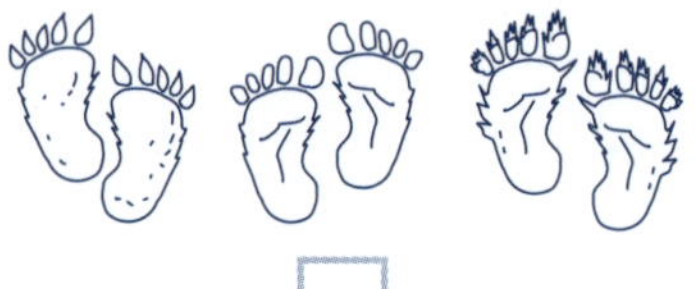

☐ It is very consistent!

Spacing

Even spacing between letters and words helps to make your handwriting legible.

Copy the text, then add the letter 'o' between each word to check your spacing.

Footprintsosupposedlyomadeoby a Yeti were seen by a mountaineer in Bhutan in 2016. His claims were later supported by a yak herder. The yak herder claimed he had seen the Yeti in the same area. He said the hairy monster stood upright, about 90 metres ahead of him.

Try stretching the space between each letter, then write them again using even spacing.

m m m   w w w   a a a   n n n

mmm

Copy the sentence. Use the columns to help you maintain even spacing.

Many people in Nepal believe that the Yeti is a nocturnal creature that growls and whistles.

Size

Practise writing words at different sizes. Write the words in the footprints.

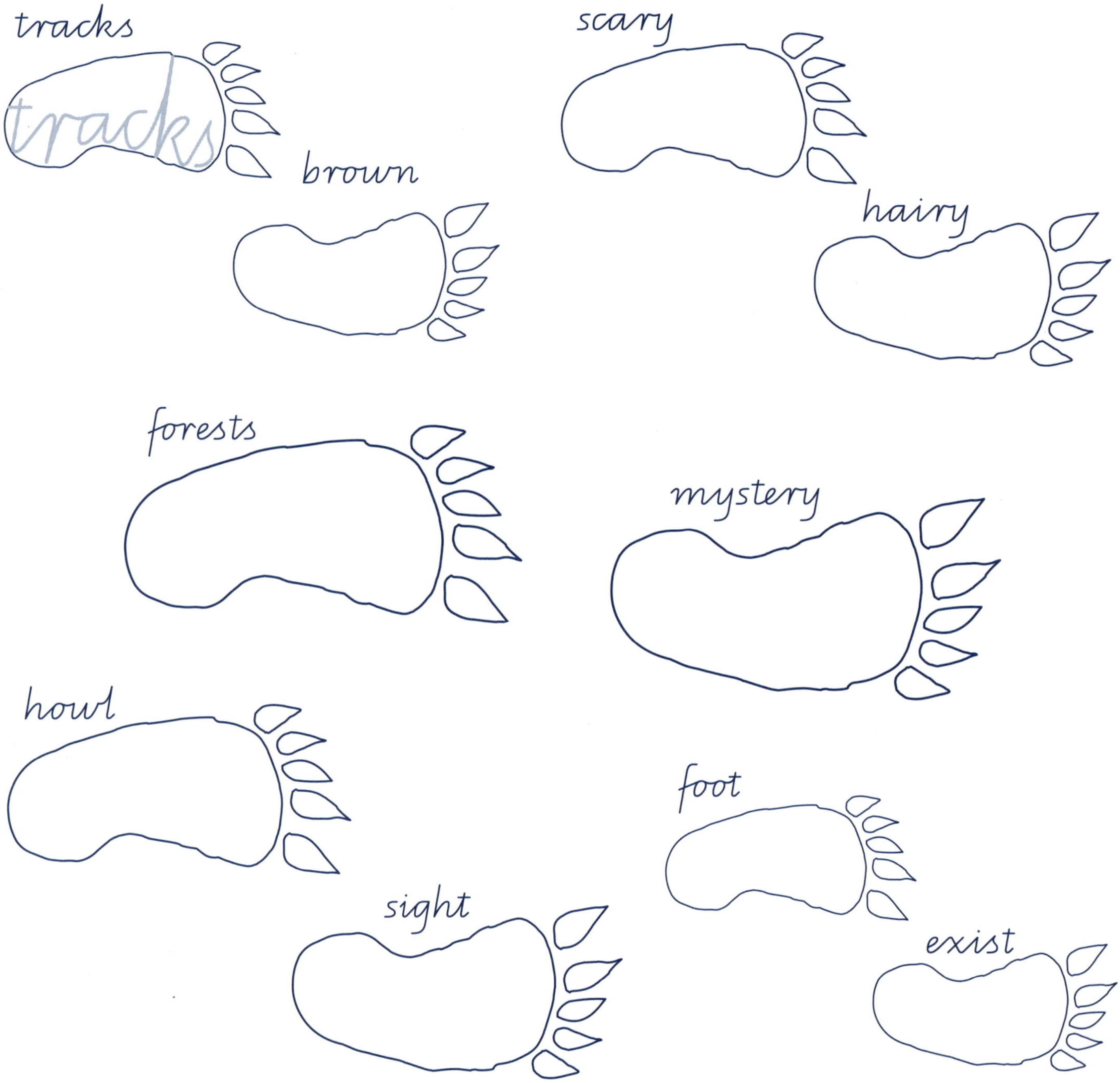

Trace the word 'Bigfoot' with letters of different sizes. Complete the second 'Bigfoot'.
Focus on forming the letters correctly.

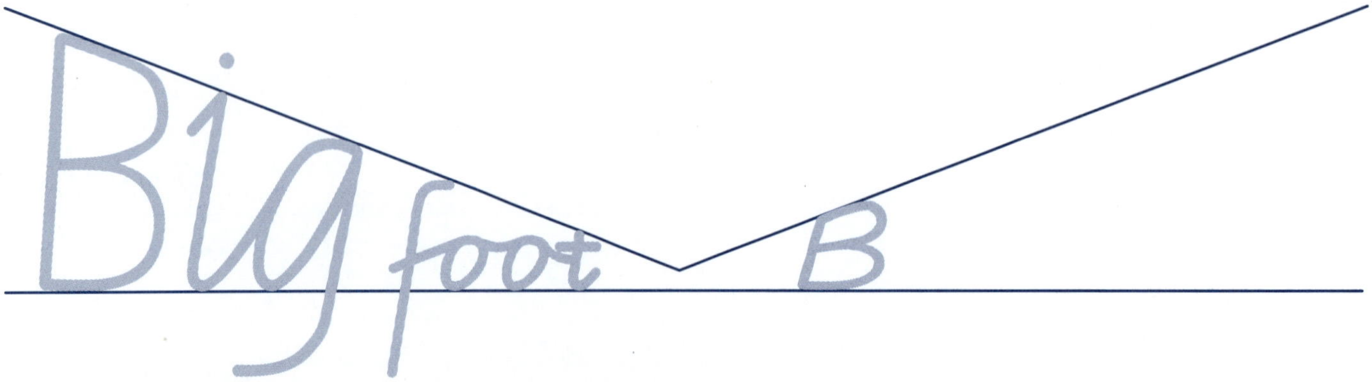

Speed and legibility

Work with a partner. How many times can you write the word 'mystery' in one minute?

Print

mystery

_____ times

Cursive

mystery

_____ times

Capital letters

MYSTERY

_____ times

My fastest script:

My neatest script:

My preferred script:

get.ga/PMWA133

End-of-module evaluation: A Yeti sighting

Copy the text, then evaluate your handwriting.

I had heard of the legend of the Yeti before I embarked on my trip to Nepal. I knew that some people claimed to have seen a Yeti, and even taken grainy photographs. I had heard about the long, large footprints. What I was not prepared for, while taking a walk not far from my accommodation, was a sighting in the distance of what could have been a Yeti. The creature appeared to be taller than me, with a shaggy, bent, ape-like back. I was not frightened, but curious, my feet frozen to the spot. I made a mental note to try to find footprints later.

Evaluation grid				
	Student		Teacher	
Letters and words are a consistent size.	☐ Yes	☐ No	☐ Yes	☐ No
Letters and words are evenly spaced.	☐ Yes	☐ No	☐ Yes	☐ No
Slope is consistent.	☐ Yes	☐ No	☐ Yes	☐ No
All joins are accurate.	☐ Yes	☐ No	☐ Yes	☐ No
Handwriting is legible.	☐ Yes	☐ No	☐ Yes	☐ No

Print script

Revise the print alphabet.

a b c d e f g h i j k l m n o p q r s t u v w x y z

Revise your print script. Convert the following words from cursive to print.

Cursive	Print
Triangle	
located	
Atlantic	
mysteriously	
disappeared	
Bermuda	

Copy the text.

The Bermuda Triangle is an area where many mysterious incidents have occurred. Dozens of ships, planes and people have disappeared under strange circumstances with no good explanation. The triangle is located off the east coast of Mexico and the United States of America, in the Atlantic Ocean. The three points of the triangle are Miami, Bermuda and San Juan.

ISBN: 9780170403924

Patterning exercises

Copy this diagram of Stonehenge.

Labelling maps

Add labels to the map using print script. Remember to use all capitals for country names.

United States of America | Cuba | Miami
Florida | San Juan | Puerto Rico | Bermuda

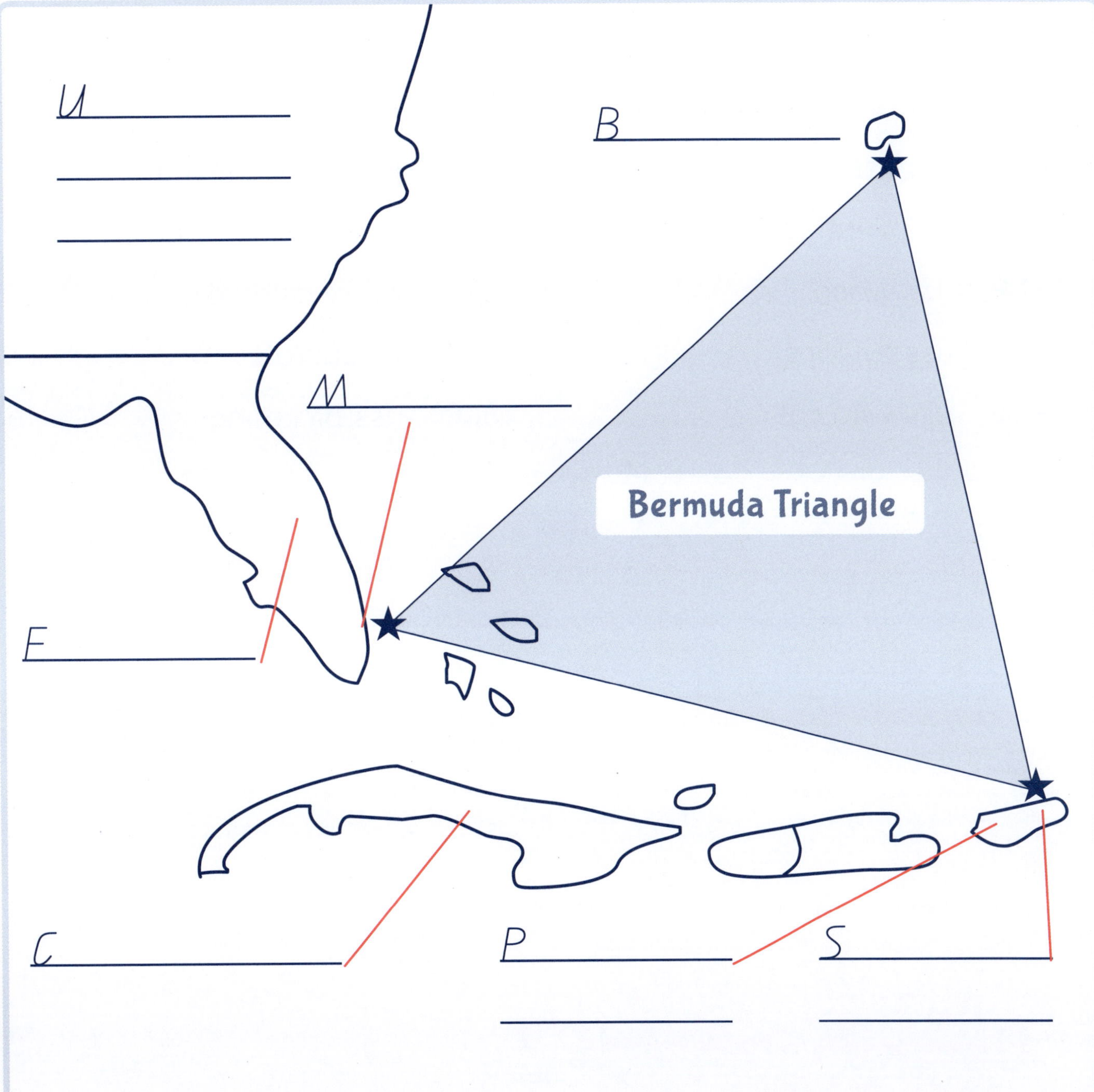

ISBN: 9780170403924

Capital letters

Revise the capital letters.

A B C D E F G H I J K L M N O P Q R S T U V

W X Y Z

Names of nautical vessels begin with capital letters. Rewrite the names of the vessels below in chronological order, using capital letters in the correct places. Watch out for acronyms.

Famous ships wrecked or missing in the Bermuda Triangle

1999	genesis	1855	james b. chester
1609	sea venture	1921	carroll a. deering
1814	uss wasp	1872	mary celeste
1918	uss cyclops	1967	witchcraft
1824	uss wild cat	1800	uss pickering

Numerals

Complete the table using print script.

Bermuda Triangle mystery	year (in numerals)	year (in words)
Christopher Colombus sees strange lights and experiences strange compass readings.	1492	fourteen ninety–two
Passenger disappears from the Patriot.		eighteen twelve
USS Epervier and crew disappear.	1815	
Crew of James B. Chester goes missing.		eighteen fifty–five
USS Proteus and USS Nereus vanish.	1941	
Flight Douglas DC–3 NC16002 disappears.		nineteen forty–eight
Marine Sulphur Queen is lost in Florida Straits.	1963	
Cabin cruiser Witchcraft goes missing.	1967	
Cargo ship Genesis and crew go missing.		nineteen ninety–nine
Cargo ship SS El Faro is wrecked, all crew go missing.		two thousand and fifteen

Revising diagonal joins

Practise these letter pairs with diagonal joins.

ai ce du ee hi ie ke lu me no ti ue xt

Underline the diagonal joins in the following words, then copy the words.

series answer inhabited triangles visible double

beautiful hundreds importantly increased statue

massive implements carefully ceremonial similar

legends complete stonework competition heavily

hidden iconic monolith volcano mysterious

Which of the following letter pairs would form a diagonal join in cursive? Circle.

ng em pu re on er ea im ge an ra le ll et

Prove your answers by writing all the letter pairs in cursive.

Self-assessment

Evaluate your use of diagonal joins.

☐ I made some mistakes.

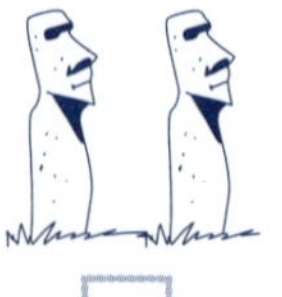

☐ Mine are very good.

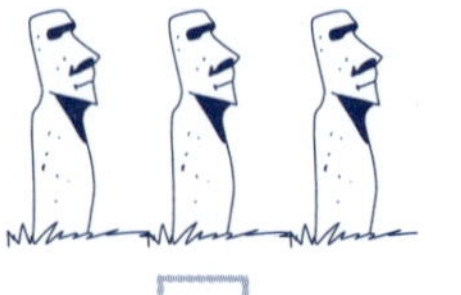

☐ Mine are excellent!

Revising 'x' joins

Practise writing the word 'waxing' in four steps.

1. wa 2. wax 3. waxin 4. waxing

1. 2. 3. 4.

Practise these 'x' words.

vexing next kick-boxing jinx equinox mixes

maximum complex boxful excavate waxed

experiment expose flexing fixable expert

Trace and copy these 'x' patterns.

xXxX xixi oxox XxXx uxux

exex xxxx

Change these 'x' words from print to cursive.

experience expression exhausted exhilaration

excluded exploration extravagant exclamation

Revising 'o' joins

Copy these words with horizontal joins from 'o'.

Remember not to dip too far.

creators icon ecosystem outdoors environmental

stone ports kilometres honour people tour torso

Copy these words with joins from 'o' to ascenders.

Remember to only retrace one-third of the ascender.

scholar isolation volcanic prohibit noble book

Copy these words.

Remember, 'o' does not join to 'e'.

shoes canoe toenail oboe echoed tomatoes does

Copy these double 'o' words.

wooden undertook afternoon overlooks seafood

schools poorly loophole woods hoops smooth

Copy the sentence.

Only two survivors were found following the shipwreck in the ocean.

Slope

Write the letters of the alphabet against the slope lines.

a b c

Write the letters of the alphabet, then draw in the slope lines using a ruler.

Copy the text, then check your slope. Use a ruler to draw in the slope lines.

Stonehenge is located in Wiltshire, England, near the town of Amesbury. It is a stark ring of standing stones. The stones are about 4 metres high and 2 metres wide. Archaeologists have calculated that the structure is over 5000 years old. There are many theories as to why and how it was built. Today, the area is roped off to prevent people from touching the stones.

get.ga/PMWA134

Spacing

Remember: correct spacing between letters and words helps with legibility.

Rewrite the text, correcting the spacing.

Ea ster Is land, or Rapa Nu i, is a s mall p iece of

land in the South Pacific. The is land is famousfor its

huge hu man-like s tatues, or moai. The statu e s

wer e ca rv ed hundreds of yearsago by Rapa Nui artists.

How the stat ues we re m oved rem ains a mystery.

How does your handwriting vary in size from the models? Copy these words in the spaces provided.

Rapa Nui   construction   moai   unknown   hilly

Polynesian   tourism   village   anchor   ancestry

Circle the word in each pair with the most even spacing.

basalt   b a s alt   quarry   quarry

ca rv ed   carved   p latfor ms   platforms

Size

Copy the words. Can you change the size of your writing and maintain your legibility?

The size at which you write can influence legibility.

disappear disappear disappear

ship ship ship ship ship

Circle a word in the size you found most comfortable to write. Underline your most legible word.

Copy the pattern. Gradually increase the size.

m m m m m

Speed and legibility

Work with a partner. How many times can you write the word 'volcano' in one minute?

Print

volcano

_____ times

Cursive

volcano

_____ times

Capital letters

VOLCANO

_____ times

My fastest script:

My neatest script:

My preferred script:

End-of-module evaluation: The Easter Island statues

Copy the text, then evaluate your handwriting.

The Easter Island statues, or moai, make a stunning sight when seen for the first time. Some soar over 10 metres high, facing inland even though they are located close to the sea. All have long heads with long ears, and upper torsos. The statues have their arms along their bodies or resting on their stomachs. There are some with eyes. The eyes are made of white and red stone and coral. A few wear hats made from scoria, a volcanic pumice stone.

Evaluation grid		
	Student	Teacher
Letters and words are a consistent size.	☐ Yes ☐ No	☐ Yes ☐ No
Letters and words are evenly spaced.	☐ Yes ☐ No	☐ Yes ☐ No
Slope is consistent.	☐ Yes ☐ No	☐ Yes ☐ No
All joins are accurate.	☐ Yes ☐ No	☐ Yes ☐ No
Handwriting is legible.	☐ Yes ☐ No	☐ Yes ☐ No

Print script

Revise the print alphabet.

a b c d e f g h i j k l m n o p q r s t u v w x y z

Revise your print script. Convert the following words from cursive.

Cursive	Print
Australia	
vanished	
surf	
recovered	
theories	
explained	

Copy the text.

Harold Holt was Prime Minister of Australia from January 1966 until his mysterious disappearance in late 1967. Holt vanished while swimming in the surf on the morning of 17 December 1967 at Cheviot Beach, near Portsea in Victoria. His body was never recovered. While there are many theories about how Holt disappeared, it's likely that he simply drowned. The Australian flag was lowered to half mast to express mourning for his loss.

Patterning exercises

Complete the patterns.

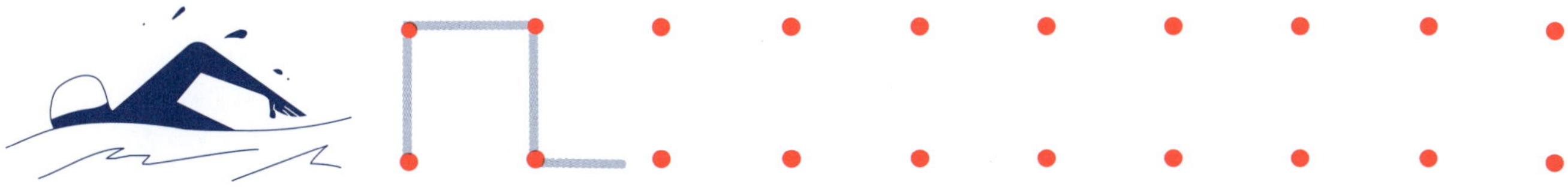

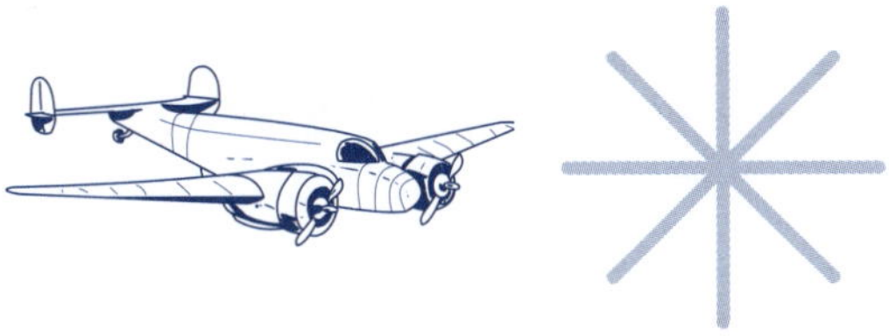

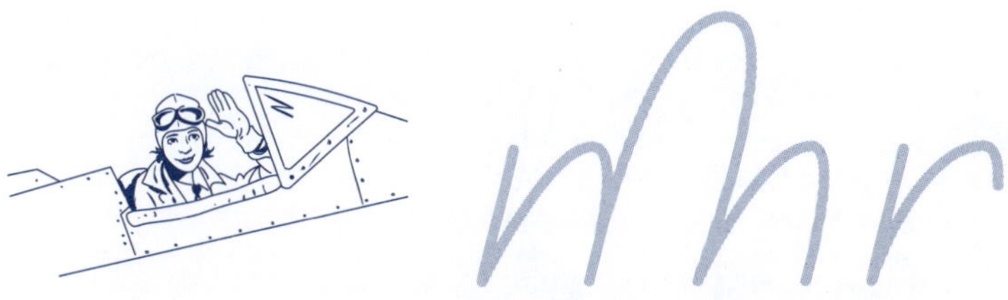

Capital letters

Revise the capital letters.

A B C D E F G H I J K L M N O P Q R S T U V

W X Y Z

Pilots use a two-letter code to abbreviate the names of countries when navigating. Copy these country names and their abbreviations.

Australia	AU	Pakistan	PK
Indonesia	ID	United States of America	US
Thailand	TH	France	FR
Papua New Guinea	PG	Puerto Rico	PR
Mexico	MX	Canada	CA
Ireland	IE	Suriname	SR
Senegal	SN	Sudan	SD

Labelling diagrams

Add labels to the diagram. Use print script.

1. landing light	2. fuel tank	3. sun blinds
4. thermometer	5. pull-up cable	6. rear cockpit

Amelia Earhart's Lockheed model 10 Electra plane

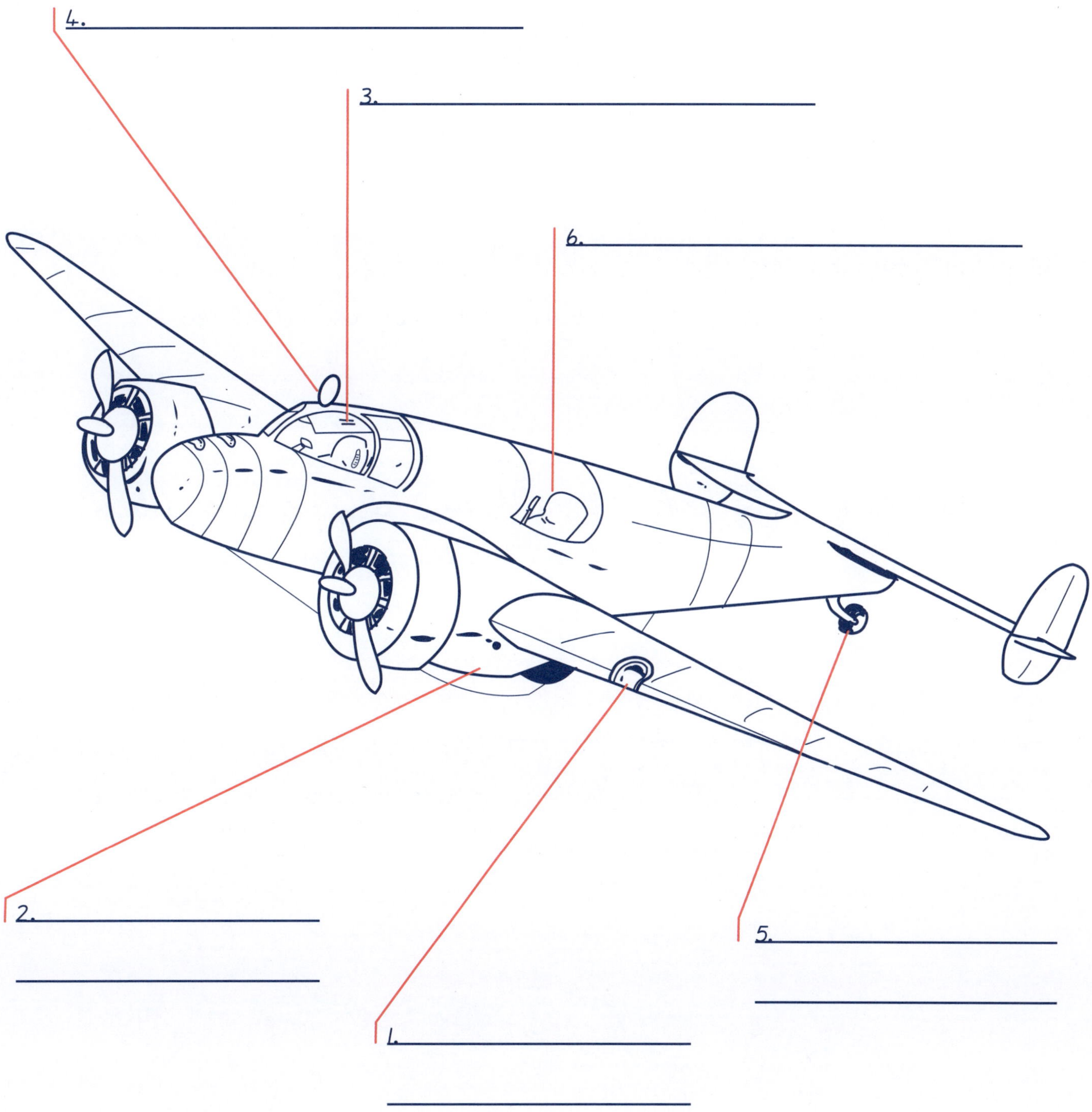

Numerals

Copy each distance in numerals and words.

Distances flown by Amelia Earhart on her final flight

Miami to San Juan	1660 km	one thousand, six hundred and sixty kilometres
San Juan to Caripito	983 km	nine hundred and eighty-three kilometres
Caripito to Paramaribo	989 km	nine hundred and eighty-nine kilometres
Paramaribo to Natal	2567 km	two thousand, five hundred and sixty-seven kilometres
Natal to St Louis	7499 km	seven thousand, four hundred and ninety-nine kilometres

Revising the letter 'r'

Remember: the letter 'r' can be joined to the next letter or left unjoined; however, it never joins to 'e'.

Copy the following letter pairs.

ra ra   ri ri   ru ru   rs rs   rt rt

Write each word twice; first with 'r' joined to the next letter, then unjoined.

Harold Harold   Victoria Victoria   friends friends

strong strong   experienced experienced   sorts sorts

drowned drowned   swimmers swimmers   early early

parliament parliament   current current

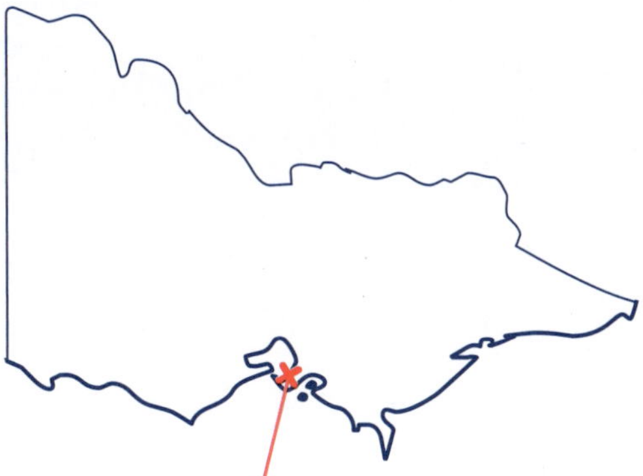

Cheviot Beach

get.ga/PMWA135

Copy the following words in which 'r' does not join to 'e'.   *re*

disappeared   bureau   creature   enquire   furore

fluorescent   fireworks   firewall   fixture   respect

distress   declared   creak   compared   caretaker

represent   bereft   barely   break   reef

Revising letters that don't join

b g j p s y z

clockwise finishers

Remember: clockwise finishers do not join to the next letter. The letter 'q' is also a letter that does not join to the next letter, as the join line would be too long.

Copy these words with letters that do not join.

aquatic disappear beach body people jagged

thought abducted collapsed year dangerous rescue

attempt figure flying biggest dizzy washed

The top finishers o, r, v and w do not join to 'e'.

Copy the following words with top finishers followed by 'e'.

went believe never remembered crewmen above

poem reconstruct represent realistic departure

nerve attractive massive extensive aggressive oboe

Put a red dot where there will be no join in cursive.

basic type speed joins capital review

every describe moved weather recount

Revising double letters

Remember: some letter pairs can be written in more than one way.

Copy these double letter pairs.

aa bb cc dd ee ff gg kk ll mm

nn oo pp rr rr ss ss tt tt uu zz

These double-letter pairs need drop-on joins. Practise them. Complete the lines.

aa dd cc

Practise these joins.

'r' can be joined or left unjoined. rr rr

Double 's' has two forms:

horizontal join oss

diagonal join ess

Double 't' – cross in one stroke or two. tt tt

Copy these words with double letters.

crossed disappear specially Lockheed Noonan

biggest suggest pattern guess common choose

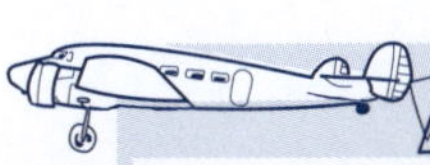

Self-assessment

My double letters:

☐ need practice.

☐ are pretty good.

☐ are great!

Slope

Practise maintaining a consistent slope. Copy each word in the slope grid.

mystery

disappear

life

career

identity

records

attempt

theories

Spacing

Copy the following text, then add the letter 'o' between each word to check your spacing.

AmeliaoEarhartoisobest known as the first female pilot

to fly across the Atlantic Ocean. Earhart was born in

Kansas, USA on 24 July 1897. In June 1937 she departed

from Miami, Florida, with her navigator Fred Noonan.

They planned to fly around the world. They mysteriously

disappeared while flying over the Pacific Ocean, from

Lae in New Guinea towards Howland Island. She was

last heard from on 2 July 1937. Amelia Earhart, her

navigator and her plane were never found.

Rewrite the following words with more appropriate spacing between the letters.

av ia tor   r ec ords   p ilot   in str ument

dep art ure   dir ection   s ign als   p os ition

dis coveries   m e moir   attempt   p lane

Size

Copy the words. Can you change the size of your writing and maintain your legibility?

never never never never

tides tides tides tides tides

Circle a word in the size you found the most comfortable to write.
Underline your most legible word.

How many times can you fit these words along the lines with no space between the words?

recovered ______ times

accidental ______ times

turbulent ______ times

mourning ______ times

swimming ______ times

Speed and legibility

Work with a partner. How many times can you write the word 'plane' in one minute?

Print

plane

_____ times

Cursive

plane

_____ times

Capital letters

PLANE

_____ times

My fastest script: ______________________________

My neatest script: ______________________________

My preferred script: ______________________________

End-of-module evaluation: Description of a rip tide

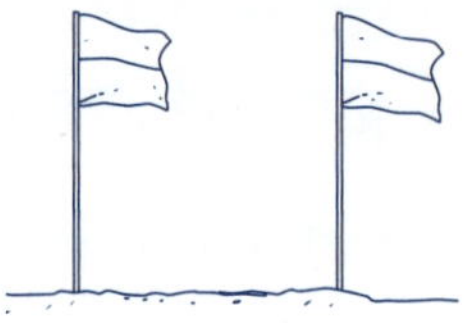

Copy the text, then evaluate your handwriting.

It is believed a rip tide played a part in Harold Holt's disappearance. Rips are our silent beach killers, as many swimmers can't identify them. Rips are strong currents that start near the shore and flow out to sea. The rip area often appears calmer and darker. Usually there is no wave activity, which deceives swimmers into thinking that it is a safe place to swim. Our surf lifesavers can read surf conditions and set up the red and yellow flags indicating a safe place to swim. The best advice, should you get caught in a rip, is to not panic, try to float and raise your arm to indicate you require assistance.

Evaluation grid

	Student		Teacher	
Letters and words are a consistent size.	☐ Yes	☐ No	☐ Yes	☐ No
Letters and words are evenly spaced.	☐ Yes	☐ No	☐ Yes	☐ No
Slope is consistent.	☐ Yes	☐ No	☐ Yes	☐ No
All joins are accurate.	☐ Yes	☐ No	☐ Yes	☐ No
Handwriting is legible.	☐ Yes	☐ No	☐ Yes	☐ No

Practising the flourished alphabet

Revise the flourished capital letters. Use the slope grids to guide you.

A A

B B

C C

D D

E E

F F

G G
1 2 H 3 H
I I
J J
1 2 K K
L L
1 2 M M

1 2 N N

O O

2 1 P P

1 2 Q Q

2 1 R R

S S

2 1 T T

U U

V V

W W

1 2
X X

Y Y

Z Z

get.ga/PMWA136

Revise the flourished lower-case letters. Use the slope grids to guide you.

a b

c d

e f

g h

i j

k l

m n

o p

q

r

s

t

u

v

w

x

y

z

Circle the flourished letters that change from cursive, then copy the flourished alphabet.

a b c d e f g h i j k l m n o p q r s
t u v w x y z

Practise forming joins with the flourished letters. Follow the steps below.

ab 1. a 2. al 3. ab

ed 1. e 2. eo 3. ed

if 1. i 2. if 3. if

th 1. t 2. tl 3. th

ok 1. o 2. ol 3. ok

il 1. i 2. il

mp 1. m 2. mj 3. mp

ax 1. an 2. ax

Using flourished script

Copy the following words in flourished script.

phenomena theories hoax

supernatural aliens

Match each word from above to a meaning. Then write the word in flourished script and copy the meaning in cursive.

creatures from other planets

something intended to deceive

scientific facts or events

cannot be explained by the laws of science or nature

ideas explaining something

Practising all scripts

Print script

a b c d e f g h i j k l m n o p q r s t u v w x y z

Queensland Modern Cursive

abcdefghijklmnopqrstuvwxyz

Capital letters and numerals

A B C D E F G H I J K L M N O P Q R S T U V

W X Y Z

0 1 2 3 4 5 6 7 8 9

Flourished alphabet

aA bB cC dD eE fF gG

hH iI jJ kK lL mM

nN oO pP qQ rR sS tT

uU vV wW xX yY zZ

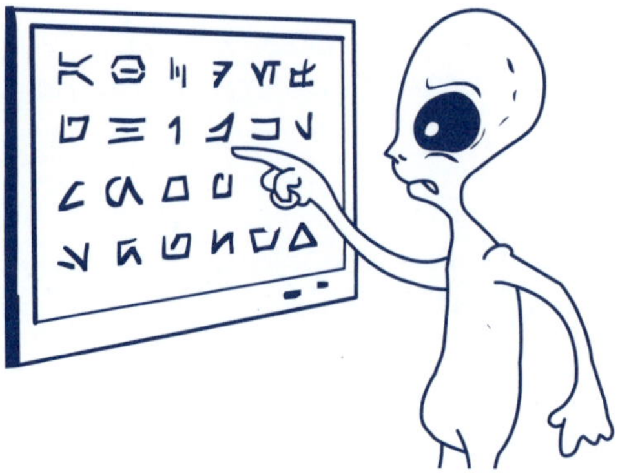

Independent writing activity

Write a short exposition to persuade your reader. You may write for or against the statement below. Use your best cursive handwriting.

Remember: a persuasive text must have:

- *a title*
- *a statement of position*
- *a series of arguments*
- *a concluding statement.*

'The search for extraterrestrial life is a waste of money.'

Teacher observation guide

Student is: left-handed ☐ right-handed ☐

Student demonstrates correct posture, paper position and pencil grip. ☐

Student forms the print alphabet with accuracy. ☐

Student forms capital letters with accuracy. ☐

Student can write numerals with accuracy. ☐

Student forms the following joins with accuracy:

- drop-on joins ☐
- joins to ascenders ☐
- 'f' joins ☐
- 's' joins ☐
- horizontal joins ☐
- diagonal joins ☐
- 'x' joins ☐
- 'o' joins ☐
- 'r' joins ☐

Student has an understanding of which letters do not join. ☐

Student uses Queensland Modern Cursive confidently. ☐

Student can convert between scripts. ☐

Student uses 8 mm writing lines with accuracy. ☐

Student has an understanding of the factors that influence legibility (slope, spacing, size, speed). ☐

Student is progressing towards a fluent and legible personal handwriting style. ☐

Notes:

....

....

....

Date:

....